THE AUTHORS CIRCLE

WRITTEN AND ILLUSTRATED BY CHARLES BONE

FOREWORD BY SIR JOHN GIELGUD

TREMLETT'S BOOKS

Published and distributed by Tremlett's Books Limited
8 Harts Yard
Godalming
Surrey, GU7 1AS

Designed by Geoffrey A.J. Butcher FCSD
Anchor House
Longcross Road
Chertsey
Surrey, KT16 0AH

Printed by BAS Printers Limited
Orange Lane
Over Wallop
Stockbridge
Hampshire, SO20 8JD

British Library cataloguing and publication data
A catalogue record of this book is available in the British Library

ISBN 0 9534100 0 5

first edition of 1000 copies
signed by the author

THE AUTHORS CIRCLE

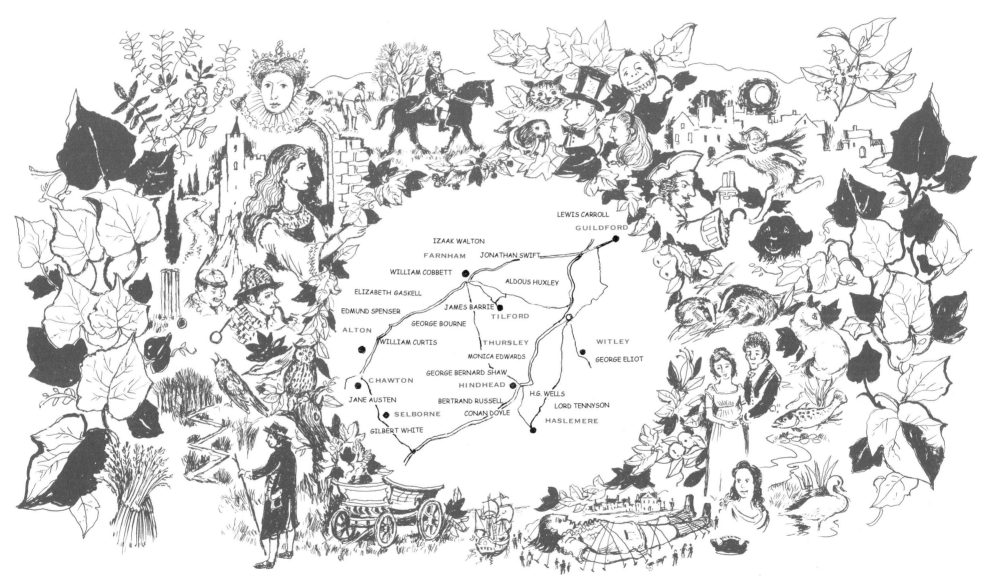

LEWIS CARROLL
GUILDFORD

IZAAK WALTON
FARNHAM   JONATHAN SWIFT
WILLIAM COBBETT   ALDOUS HUXLEY
ELIZABETH GASKELL
EDMUND SPENSER   JAMES BARRIE
                         TILFORD
ALTON   GEORGE BOURNE
          WILLIAM CURTIS   THURSLEY   WITLEY
                         MONICA EDWARDS   GEORGE ELIOT
          CHAWTON   GEORGE BERNARD SHAW
                    HINDHEAD
JANE AUSTEN   BERTRAND RUSSELL   H.G. WELLS
          SELBORNE   CONAN DOYLE   LORD TENNYSON
GILBERT WHITE   HASLEMERE

FOREWORD 5
INTRODUCTION 6

JANE AUSTEN 8
JAMES BARRIE 10
GEORGE BOURNE 12
LEWIS CARROLL 14
WILLIAM COBBETT 16
WILLIAM CURTIS 18
ARTHUR CONAN DOYLE 20
MONICA EDWARDS 22
GEORGE ELIOT 24
ELIZABETH GASKELL 26
ALDOUS HUXLEY 28
BERTRAND RUSSELL 30
GEORGE BERNARD SHAW 32
EDMUND SPENSER 34
JONATHAN SWIFT 36
ALFRED LORD TENNYSON 38
IZAAK WALTON 40
H G WELLS 42
GILBERT WHITE 44

INDEX 46

FOREWORD

Following 'Charles Bone's Waverley', involved with the history of towns and villages in the area, this book is concerned with authors of international reputation who lived or worked in this very small part of the South of England.

I remember the countryside with great affection. My elder brother was friendly with Aldous Huxley and I recall our association in school days at Hillside, near Godalming.

Charles Bone has written and illustrated this book to record the association in the locality of these authors as information of this sort can easily be lost.

Sir John Gielgud

INTRODUCTION

This book began, as many things do, at Surrey University. At a preview of an art exhibition, I was discussing authors with some of the students. None of them came from these parts and did not realise the number of writers of international importance that had lived or had connections in this area.

As I began to research, more came to light. Its relative proximity to London, yet still peaceful and rural, made this part of Southern England an attractive environment for creative work. In George Eliot's day, Witley was only one hour's train journey to London - then the centre of the publishing world. Today authors might seek their solitude further afield, but the area is still essentially rural although Cobbett's great Wen moves closer by the day.

Taking Farnham as a central point, the authors' houses I have illustrated here are all within a 20 minute drive. Some are now schools, nursing homes, hotels and public houses and some are still private houses. The homes of Jane Austen and Gilbert White are open to the public at certain times of the year.

If any one person can be said to have drawn creative talent to the Author's Circle, in particular to Hindhead and Haslemere , it is Anne Gilchrist, writer and biographer. After her husband died, Anne coudn't afford to stay in London and moved to Brook Bank, Shottermill near Haslemere, to live in a cottage surrounded by heather and hills.

When Anne wasn't writing she was bringing up four children and would visit her mother in Earls Colne, Essex for several months at a time and rent her cottage. This had a particular appeal to authors because of her fine collection of books and pictures and many well-known writers experienced their first taste of the area staying in Shottermill. Attracted by the beauty of this corner of the Surrey and Hampshire borders, it wasn't long before they were either frequent visitors or had invested in property here themselves.

The history of literature in the area begins with Waverley, which was the first Cistercian Abbey in England, a large complex visited by Kings, Queens and Bishops and their retinues. Like all religious orders scribes and bookbinders plied their trade in the abbey workshops. Before the invention of printing, all manuscripts were copied and illustrated by hand and the books were very valuable and rare. Authors did not receive royalties or any finance for the actual sale of books, but did receive a grant or award from some prominent person.

In the handwritten duplication of the text, much of the original was distorted, sometimes for religious or political reasons, and often by accident, and so the original book became adapted and the identity of the author often lost. A book might have taken years to produce, yet some 200 sheep had donated their skins!

Since the majority of the population could not read, books were read by groups of scholars. Monks could loan from the abbey library one book for one year to be returned in 12 months finished or not. The price of a book might be the equivalent of a year's pay.

Now of course the price of a best-selling paperback is not much different from the minimum hourly wage. Almost everyone can read, and bookshops and libraries are full of a wide and enticing range of the new and the not so new. Books are affordable and available.

Compared to the Victorians, as we approach the Millennium our technology and pace of life makes demands which render the simple act of reading very low on many lists. Our attention span gets ever shorter and our imagination, titillated to bursting point, is no longer the most personal of creations.

Before television, before personal computers, and before the Internet, there was time to read, time to notice and time to respond. Before the railway, before telephones, and before the motor car, there was time to read. Before the printing press there was time to read but hardly any books and few could afford to buy them.

It speaks volumes for the earliest writers featured in this book that they achieved greatness when few could access the words they were uttering. Since then many authors and creative talents have chosen to spend time within this notional Authors' Circle. They became part of a long literary and artistic tradition, establishing a convivial atmosphere away from politics and urban depravation, where illness might be cured, depression eased and a wilderness enjoyed.

JANE AUSTEN
1775-1817

The house at Chawton near Alton where Jane Austen lived for the last eight happy and productive years of her life is now a museum. It has rather refined features, built of timber and handmade local brick sometime before 1712, and is listed in the National Archives as a building of historic interest.

Jane lived here with her inseparable sister Cassandra and mother from 1809 to 1817. It was here that she revised her novels *Sense and Sensibility*, *Pride and Prejudice* and *Northanger Abbey*. *Mansfield Park*, *Emma*, and *Persuasion* were all written at Chawton.

Jane Austen had a strange arrangement with her publisher, being liable for the loss if any novel did not make a profit. It never happened but the most Jane ever made from her writings was just £808.

The rooms in the house are quite small and somewhat austere, but the house has a quiet atmosphere and one can imagine that Jane had the time and space, and certainly the peace necessary to develop her novels and letters.

With her interest in music she soon installed a piano and she was a very adept needlewoman. While sewing or working on tapestries she would often get up and note down some feature in her plot, which would later develop into the intricate relationships we have come to know in her books. The Austens were a united family and two of her six brothers had successful careers in the Navy. Admiral Sir Francis Austen became Admiral of the Fleet.

In spite of their travels to London, Hampshire and Bath, they always kept in constant touch. Jane's third brother Edward inherited Goldmersham Park in Kent from cousins and the estates in Hampshire, and it was through his initiative that the cottage now famous as Jane Austen's house was made available to the family.

The house was accepted without any previous inspection since on earlier visits to the Alton area it was the part of England that they most liked. It was considered that the house was as good as some parsonage houses of the time. In Jane's day the house was on the main Winchester road, but now it enjoys the peace and tranquility of a country lane. Still in the outhouse lies the donkey carriage used by the two sisters for their shopping visits to nearby Alton.

The house displays original letters, illustrations to Jane's books and some of the original furniture and, upstairs, a display of fashion of the period. The house also has a small bookshop with a comprehensive selection of her novels.

Before the Austens lived here the house was used by the bailiff of Chawton House, and at one time it was the New Inn. After Cassandra's death in 1845 the house enjoyed very little attention for 100 years until the late Dorothy Darnell established the Jane Austen Society in 1940. Through their introduction a Mr T. Edward Carpenter purchased the house in memory of his son killed in action in 1944, vesting the building in the Jane Austen Memorial Trust, opening it as a museum in 1949.

JANE AUSTEN'S HOUSE

JAMES BARRIE
1860-1937

It was James Barrie's passion for cricket which led him in 1900 to purchase a house in the Tilford area known as Black Lake Cottage. Barrie had a cricket team called the *Allah-Akbarries* or 'may the Lord help us' in Arabic. Matches were played on the famous Tilford cricket green and were most entertaining events. They usually featured Abbey, the Royal academician, A E W Mason the novelist, Blomfield the architect and, of course, the star performer, Conan Doyle, the fast bowler of the group.

Barrie was one of Conan Doyle's oldest friends. Not only did they collaborate on an operetta, they were both intrigued by psychic phenomena. Barrie was convinced of the authenticity of the renowned early photographs of fairies, said by specialists to be genuine. Years later, near the end of her life, one of the 'fairies' admitted they were fakes and remembered posing for the photographs when a child.

Black Lake Cottage was extended under the direction of Mrs Barrie, who would organise extensive weekend parties for the cricketers. When he wasn't playing cricket her husband was writing and much of *Quality Street, The Admirable Crichton* and *Peter Pan* was created at the cottage between 1900 and 1904. In the 1970s the cottage became the Lobswood Club and has since been extended further. It is now privately owned.

When the Llewellyn Davies family came to stay at another nearby cottage they brought with them their two sons Peter and Michael. They were friends of Barrie, a brilliant storyteller, and so he began his stories to the boys on the shores of Black Lake Pond, which he described as a South Sea lagoon. Red Indians and fairies lived on the banks, and though the intensity of his concentrated descriptions bordered on the alarming at times, this area became important to Barrie as part of the inspirational force for the creator of *Peter Pan*.

Barrie was a keen croquet player and constructed a lawn on the south side of the building. In June 1901 the Barries purchased a steam car, which proved very unreliable although it achieved 20 mph, quite a speed for the time. It proved to be serviceable for the summer months only as the chauffeur had many mechanical failures and punctures to deal with, leaving the passengers stranded, sometimes in remote parts.

James' older brother David had died at the age of 14, when his younger brother was only six, and David's memory is reflected in much of Barrie's work, forever the first 'boy who would not grow up'. And when Barrie staged his 1936 production of *The Boy David* a year before his death, it appeared to be about the King David of the Bible, but it was really about his long lost brother.

BLACK LAKE COTTAGE

GEORGE BOURNE
1863-1927

George Bourne took his name from the village of Bourne where he chose to live in 1900 at Vine Cottage with his two unmarried sisters. His real name was George Sturt, owner of the wheelwright's business at 84 East Street, Farnham. He adopted the pseudonym in order to disguise his literary work as he felt that writing would be misconstrued by townspeople as damaging to his business reputation.

Happy that he was suitably protected, he wrote a series of articles for *Country Life*, and *The Memoirs of a Surrey Labourer*. Other authors such as Henry Williamson had a great admiration for his books, since they are a true record of rural life at the time.

In *Surrey Labourer* Bourne was in fact writing about Fred Bettesworth, a pseudonym for Freddie Grover, his odd-job man and gardener. Freddie had been a farm labourer all his life, reflecting the lot of the working man in villages throughout the country. It came then as something of a shock to discover that his gardener had served in the Crimean War.

Bourne was influenced by William Morris and studied briefly at a local art school, eventually becoming a governor, and ever since his early days as a student teacher he maintained a strong interest in education, mourning the squandering of poor people's talents. George was well connected in literary circles, and it was Arnold Bennett who encouraged him to write a regular journal. So regular did it become that it ran to 4,000 sheets. They remained locked away for many years and were not published until 1967.

With the outbreak of the Great War many of his employees were called to the front but George was unable to enlist as he suffered from severe asthma. He stopped writing at the age of 50 and the wheelwright's business also became too much for him and was sold. His contribution to the study of old Surrey dialect should not be overlooked. This was written in phonetic form and is now the only evidence of the old dialect.

The Wheelwright's Shop, written in 1923 when his health was in a poor state, is considered the pinnacle of his achievement, a record of a vanishing craft and a way of life long gone.

VINE COTTAGE

LEWIS CARROLL
1832-1898

After the death of his father and because he had several friends in the Guildford area, Lewis Carroll looked for a house in West Surrey. G Portal, a school friend from Rugby and the Rector of Albury, helped Lewis in his search. In consultation with his sisters he finally decided on Chestnuts. Leased from 1868 to 1898 by Carroll for £73 a year, it was the view of the River Wey and the valley that finally met with the approval of the family.

Lewis Carroll, or to give him his real name The Reverend Charles Lutwidge Dodgson, considered Chestnuts to be his home, always returning to see his six sisters as frequently as possible, particularly at Christmas time.

The family were heavily involved with various local events in Guildford and in 1869 Lewis Carroll began to support amateur dramatics. He had a very wide circle of friends including Holman Hunt, Rossetti and Millais, and Arthur Hughes from whom he purchased paintings.

Queen Victoria enjoyed *Alice's Adventures in Wonderland* and probably read the copy presented to her eight year old daughter Princess Beatrice. The original title page by Tenniel is now on view at the Huntington Library in Los Angeles. Published in 1865, it was followed seven years later by the sequel *Through the Looking-Glass*. Carroll also wrote humorous verse like *The Hunting of the Snark*.

Carroll became a close friend of Ellen Terry, the actress, who he first saw in a performance of *A Winter's Tale* at the age of eight. The pair remained good friends, Lewis photographing her and visiting her frequently. He was a gifted photographer and there are plenty of examples of his work, some in the Guildford Museum.

Most particular over the production of his books, he would keep an eye on the financial outlay and production to the point of causing great concern to the publishers, Macmillan, and also to the printers.

When he died, aged 65, Carroll's coffin was carried from Chestnuts to St. Mary's Parish Church, where Canon Grant and Dr Paget, Dean of Christchurch, conducted the funeral.

At the age of 14 Audrey Fuller was one of the Victorian children who loved and admired Lewis Carroll. She it was who suggested the children might collect enough money to subscribe to a permanent cot in the Great Ormond Street Hospital. The St. James Gazette gathered the subscriptions and the £1,000 required for a permanent bed was secured. One cannot imagine a more suitable memorial to this remarkable man.

CHESTNUTS

WILLIAM COBBETT
1762-1835

In William Hazlitt's famous essay *The Spirit of the Age* devoted to Cobbett in 1831, he said that the author of over 40 books and originator of Hansard, 'is not only unquestionably the most powerful political writer of his time but one of the best writers in the language'.

William Cobbett was born in Farnham and lived at the Jolly Farmer Inn, now named after him. As a young man he worked for the Bishop in the Farnham Castle gardens where a growing fascination for things botanical led him to walk all the way to the Royal Gardens at Kew in order to study the plants.

It was of great concern to Cobbett that the ancient gardens of the monks of Waverley were destroyed by Robert Rich in the building of his new house and garden. The original monks' garden had produced the finest plums, peaches and apricots but the land was reduced to a coarse meadow when Waverley Abbey House was developed.

In his book *The English Garden* Cobbett's political views reflect the conditions of agricultural workers of the time but led him to not only spend two years in Newdigate Prison for writing a condemnation of army flogging, but also two periods of self-imposed exile in America though he continued writing pro-British pamphlets there under the pseudonym 'Peter Porcupine'. He also edited *The Political Register,* containing many of his important writings between 1802 and 1835.

Cobbett joined the 54th Foot for eight years rising to regimental sergeant major and afterwards became MP for Malden. William had some sympathy with the Luddite machine breakers and confessed, 'I never like to see machines lest I be tempted to understand them.'

Rural Rides, his great horseback journey in the 1820s was his greatest achievement, a powerful record of old rural England long since disappeared. His descriptions, both angry and perceptive, of early nineteenth century farmworkers' lives are unique and, because he cared so deeply about the countryside he would become politically involved.

Cobbett was a keen follower of the Harriers but after receiving a lash from a huntsman's whip and intent on revenge, he dragged a herring over Sele (now Seale) Common into a swamp. With their hounds following the scent into the mud and slime, the huntsmen had to dismount in deep mud and had great difficulty retrieving the hounds, much to the pleasure of William Cobbett, watching from a safe distance.

William Cobbett died on a farm in Normandy, north of the Hog's Back, an area famous for its fine views. Before he died, a yeoman to the end, he asked to be carried through his beloved fields to see his crops one last time. Many of his artefacts and original letters can be seen in the Cobbett collection at the museum of Farnham.

THE WILLIAM COBBETT

WILLIAM CURTIS
1746-1799

William Curtis' developed an early passion for all aspects of natural history. He became apprenticed at the age of just 14 to his grandfather, a surgeon-apothecary but realised his natural vocation as he became an avid reader of anything about exotic plants. In 1781 he started the *Botanical Magazine* which was still being published two centuries later, having a lasting influence on the design and development of some of the great English gardens.

The Curtis family lived in Lenten Street, Alton in a house built in 1702 which has since been enlarged. As a young man William was friendly with John Legg the ostler of the Crown Inn, and it was John who whetted the budding botanist's enthusiasm for collecting specimens and the science of flora.

By the time he was 20 it was decided he would complete his medical education in London and though Dr Curtis soon inherited a well established practice, his heart was still in botany, so he sold it. With support from two brothers of the Reverend Gilbert White, the distinguished naturalist of Selborne, he started a small botanical garden in Bermondsey, later another in Lambeth Marsh.

Curtis major work, certainly the one he spent the most time over, was the monumental *Flora Londinensis* which though magnificently illustrated was not a financial success. Each number contained six folio plates and many pages of letterpress, giving the Latin names of the plants illustrated and details of their history and the insects which they harboured.

There were three production stages. First, the water colour drawings were produced by the two principal artists Sydenham Edwards and James Sowerby. Engravings were then produced from the paintings, most of them by Francis Sanson. All the illustrations were hand coloured by a team of young ladies, each with a specific colour to complete on every plate, under the direction of William Graves of Wandsworth, a close friend of Curtis. Examples of this work can be seen in the Curtis Museum at Alton.

The William Curtis legacy to the wild flora of London lives on. When a second world war bomb site was cleared it was developed as an ecological park and named after him. When Curtis died his son Thomas took over the running of the magazine, but it became truly established thanks to his nephew Samuel Curtis. The first number appeared in 1781 and during William's lifetime 2,000 copies of each number were sold.

In 1782 there was a panic over the numbers of brown-tailed moths. Parish officers offered rewards for killing them and attended to make sure they were burnt. It was thought they were forerunners of the Plague and prayers were offered. It was Curtis who determined to make a careful study of the caterpillar and his published findings showed there was no cause for alarm. The William Curtis influence on botanical development and conservation is unique.

LENTEN STREET, ALTON

ARTHUR CONAN DOYLE
1859-1930

Conan Doyle authorised his friend, architect and spiritualist Henry Ball of Southsea, to design and oversee the building of Undershaw. The house, now the Undershaw Restaurant and Hotel on the A3 at Hindhead, is approached by a long bush- and tree-lined drive. It is also very steep and, on one occasion, Conan Doyle had a narrow escape when his car mounted the bank and overturned, only the steering column preventing him being crushed.

Conan Doyle's wife Louise had long suffered from tuberculosis and when he learnt from his novelist friend Grant Allen that the dry and sheltered Hindhead air helped him recover from the disease, he visited the area and immediately took to it. It was 1897 and Conan Doyle was about to enjoy life as a true sporting country gentleman, with four stallions and two saddle-mares stabled close by. In his autobiography, he refers to this time of his life as 'an interlude of peace'.

Built below the level of the main London to Portsmouth highway, the well sheltered building was designed with an abundance of windows, including the stained glass ones in the hall bearing the Doyle family's coat of arms. Inside there would be a wood-panelled drawing room full of Conan Doyle's travel souvenirs and a large billiard room.

Born in Edinburgh, unlike many young qualified doctors of today, Conan Doyle had a lot of time on his hands and spent it reading detective stories. This had become an absorbing interest but he was appalled by the standard of the work and so began writing stories based on his own observation and medical knowledge. Sherlock

Holmes and Doctor Watson had arrived! It was his medical knowledge, put to good use in the Boer War in the field hospital at Bloemfontein, which resulted in a knighthood in 1902.

Conan Doyle also had a fascination for the supernatural, perhaps inherited, perhaps acquired in childhood, which he shared with his close friend Sir James Barrie. He was to famously champion the existence of fairies, as shown in photographs taken by two Yorkshire girls. But it was also their interest in cricket that brought them together. A fine all-round sportsman, Conan Doyle played for the MCC and once bowled out W G Grace, recording his achievement in verse.

Conan Doyle was good at boxing, billiards and lawn tennis. He was elected a life member of the National Rifle Association and created the local Undershaw Rifle Club with over 100 members meeting every week at his house. Targets were positioned around the estate and the members, in bush hats and decorative badges, would turn this quiet corner of Surrey into a firing range.

In 1916 Conan Doyle announced his conversion to spiritualism, the 'psychic religion' which permeated the rest of his life. Here he tried to reconcile the conflict of science and religion, culminating in his two-volume study *The History of Spiritualism* in 1926. But it is the 60 Sherlock Holmes stories which will be remembered most, often the hero being more real than his creator. When Doyle was married to his second wife Jean, the Buenos Aires Standard ran the headline 'Sherlock Holmes quietly married'.

UNDERSHAW

MONICA EDWARDS
1912-1998

Monica Edwards wrote two series of childrens' books, one set in Romney Marsh based on her own vicarage childhood at Rye Harbour in the 1940s and 50s, the other in the Devil's Punchbowl. Born at Belper in Derbyshire, she moved with her parents to Sussex and when not at school, Monica would spend days with the fishermen of Rye, her friendship with the men giving her a broader education than any school. She stored her memory with impressions that later filled her books. Her achievement as an author spanned some 35 books and a film script.

Storm Ahead (1963) was based on a disaster in 1928 when the Rye Harbour lifeboat was lost with all her 17 young crew, an event which shattered the community. Other books in the Romney Marsh series which chronicled the adventures of Tamzin Grey, concerned smuggling and the rescue of oiled seabirds.

Monica and her husband Bill had wanted to live in a more rural environment and in 1947 they heard that the 70-acre Punch Bowl Farm near Thursley was to be auctioned, but by all accounts the 17th century building was in a poor state of repair.

While she read the auction catalogue Monica became enthralled with the romantic names of properties like Hunters Field and Upper Six Acres. She was so busy reading when the bidding commenced that her first bid was enough to purchase the property without any real intention of buying at all. Monica based the first of her Punchbowl stories on this 'accidental' purchase in her 1950 *Black Hunting Whip*.

Her children were delighted with their new home in spite of the fact it had no mains water, no light, no bathroom and a privy at the bottom of the garden and very extensive dry rot. Even with all these deficiencies the place was still sheer magic for the Edwards family, not only did her husband take to farming as though born to it, she found her new environment ideal to develop her next 11 novels.

While the family busied itself scraping beams and painting walls, even taking time to wind up water from the 107 foot well shaft, Monica set about her new plots concerning buried treasure (*Frenchman's Secret*) or time travel (*Spirit of Punchbowl Farm*). She was voted Children's Author of the Year in 1960, an honour she shared with Captain WE Johns of *Biggles* fame.

Her autobiographical adult books charted her life after buying Punch Bowl Farm. *The Cats of Punchbowl Farm*, *The Badgers of Punchbowl Farm*, *The Valley and the Farm* and *Badger Valley* followed her interest in wildlife. Her field notes, from 1965 to 1979, log the hundreds of night hours spent watching and photographing badgers.

After many idyllic years there was an unfortunate accident, described in *The Valley and the Farm*, when a tractor jack-knifed and rolled over Monica's husband Bill, leaving him with multiple injuries. He slowly returned to health but he could not return to the arduous life of farming. They had no option but to sell the house and planning permission was granted to build a small house on adjacent land overlooking the farm. In spite of her failing sight, Monica continued to take her daily walk through the valley which she left to the Woodland Trust before she died.

PUNCH BOWL FARM

GEORGE ELIOT
1819-1880

The girl from a farming family in Nuneaton became a very famous Victorian figure, perhaps England's finest woman novelist. Christened Mary Ann Evans she later became George Eliot, the George being appropriated from George Sands the one time lover of Chopin.

Author of *Middlemarch, Silas Marner* and *The Mill on the Floss*, among many other works, her circle of friends included Browning, Tennyson, Burne Jones, Clara Schumann and the sculptor Princess Louise, Marchioness of Lorne.

Victorian society assumed wrongly that George Henry Lewes, a married man, and George Eliot were man and wife. In December 1876 they purchased The Heights country house at Witley for £4,950. Its proximity to the station attracted them, a fine country house with eight acres of land and a good friend living next door, the son of the physician Sir Henry Holland.

George Eliot and Lewes were intensely happy at Witley, taking walks before breakfast and playing lawn tennis. There was though a great conflict in her personality. Profoundly religious when young, she replaced her early Calvinism with her avowed humanism. She was a very sensitive person, unable to handle criticism. George Henry would screen all negative comments on her work., but it was a successful relationship, their elopement had lasted 24 years.

Tennyson the Poet Laureate lived a few miles away and he turned up several times to read to George Eliot and, on one occasion, read a section of the *Idylls of a King*, which reduced his listener to tears. The friendship between them deepened and they both attended the wedding of Tennyson's youngest son Lionel to Eleanor Locker at Westminster Abbey. However, they held different political views, Tennyson approving of colonialism and imperialism and the superiority of the English way of life, George rejecting his over simplistic view of the so-called 'backward countries'.

George Henry Lewes died in 1878 and with extensive legal complications following his death, Eliot felt unable to continue at Witley. A long period of mourning followed, but she slowly returned to normal encouraged by her friend John Cross, who did much to handle the day to day affairs and complicated financial arrangements.

A close friendship developed and they married on the 6 May 1880 at St. George's Church, Hanover Square. So the girl christened as Mary Ann Evans was now Mrs John Walter Cross, her legal name. After a series of illnesses she finally died from a heart attack just past her 61st birthday.

A lengthy debate followed whether she should or should not be buried in Westminster Abbey, her final resting place becoming Highgate Cemetery in North London. Although not buried in Poet's Corner with the other great figures of literature, George Eliot is an important part of England's literary tradition.

THE HEIGHTS

ELIZABETH GASKELL
1810-1865

Mrs Elizabeth Gaskell was mostly associated with Cheshire and the city of Manchester. Born in 1810 in the village of Knutsford she was admired by her contemporaries Carlyle, Dickens and George Eliot.

Her best known novels include *Mary Barton, Cranford and Wives and Daughters*. However, the biography of her friend Charlotte Bronte is regarded as her greatest achievement, written immediately after Bronte's death at the request of her father.

She married William, a Unitarian Minister in 1832 and together they undertook a great deal of philanthropic activity to alleviate the conditions of the poor in Manchester. Although a famous literary figure of her time she could still be found working away in the poorest areas of the city, and much of this experience and environment is reflected in her novels.

With such a demanding life her health began to deteriorate and during a trip to Paris she developed what is believed to be a serious heart condition. Undaunted, the ailing Mrs Gaskell put her own problems to one side and instead planned the purchase of a house in the country as a surprise retirement present for her husband.

At Holybourne, a village near Alton in the beautiful Hampshire countryside and well above sea level, she found an early Georgian house in more than three acres of grounds, the ideal place to complete her next novel *Wives and Daughters*. The purchase was not to be straightforward however. In the 19th century it was illegal for a wife to buy property without the consent of her husband and so Mrs Gaskell asked her son in law, a lawyer, to negotiate on her behalf the purchase of The Lawn, now known as The Lawn's Nursing Home.

Her daughters had been a great help in the frequent house-hunting excursions, operating in discrete secrecy. Unfortunately, after the purchase Elizabeth's health began to deteriorate further and she died before enjoying the retirement she and her husband so richly deserved. Her husband William was totally unaware that Elizabeth had arranged the purchase of the house, only discovering the truth after her death.

On Sunday 12 November 1865 Mrs Gaskell had attended afternoon church in the village, returning to her new home with her daughters and other visitors for a celebratory tea. But then, in mid conversation, seeming to be in such good spirits since her arrival in Hampshire, she collapsed and died instantly. Just how her writing would have been influenced by an uninterrupted life in the South is, sadly, something we will never know.

THE LAWN

ALDOUS HUXLEY
1894-1963

Aldous Huxley was born in Godalming, the third son of Leonard and Julia Huxley. His father was assistant master at Charterhouse, the school founded in 1611 on the site of a Carthusian Monastery in London and moved to Godalming in the building designed by Sir Giles Gilbert Scott in 1872.

As a child he was taken to the unveiling of a sculpture of his grandfather on a site at the Natural History Museum in London. The ceremony was performed by HRH The Prince of Wales. Later his mother founded Prior's Field Girls School near Godalming.

The school opened on the 23 January 1902 with seven girls, one boarder who insisted on bringing her dog, one day girl, three teachers and Aldous. Charles Voysey designed the bookplate and the school motto 'we live by admiration, hope and love'. The building was a combination of private house and school.

Voysey also designed the house itself with its 25 acres of garden. Within two years of its opening the number of pupils had risen to 50, Conan Doyle's daughter being one of the children. Mrs Huxley was evidently well loved by the children, not least by Aldous who spent nine years there.

In 1903 Aldous, with his cousin Gervas, was sent to Hillside, a preparatory school near Godalming. A close friendship developed with Lewis Gielgud, Sir John's elder brother, and this association continued through much of his life.

Aldous loved to cycle in and around the Punch Bowl and became very familiar with most of the area covered by this book. He left Hillside in June 1908 and went on to Eton as a King's Scholar and then to Oxford. Summers though were spent at Prior's Field.

Huxley was very much part of the cultural scene of the time, meeting DH Lawrence many times and attending the parties given by Lady Ottoline at an Elizabethan manor house near Oxford, where guests included Virginia Woolf, Mark Girtler and Robert Graves. Bertrand Russell would attend with his raucous laughter and giant ego and members of the Bloomsbury Group, Duncan Grant and Clive Bell.

Aldous painted a lot throughout his career, but in 1931 he began writing his book *Bad Utopia*. He admitted it started as a little fun at H G Wells' expense but it developed into something more. It was now 1939 and Aldous signed with MGM for the film script of *Pride and Prejudice*. His work was highly valued by the film company and he was told that they would always have work for him if he wanted it. His relationship with the media however was a stormy one and it is fair to say the press hated him.

Brave New World sold 13,000 copies in its first year here in England and 10,000 the year after, but it was never very popular in America.

His mother and father are buried in the churchyard at Compton, one of the finest churches in the area, quite near to the Watts Memorial Chapel.

PRIOR'S FIELD

BERTRAND RUSSELL
1872-1970

Bertrand Russell's involvement in the Surrey and Hampshire borders starts with his uncle and aunt. Both came to love the Hindhead and Haslemere area so much that they each had houses built here.

Lady Agatha, Bertie's aunt, first came to the Haslemere hills in 1874 with her brother Rollo when their parents rented Aldworth from the Tennysons for several months. It was Uncle Rollo, himself a poet and with some influence on the young Bertie, who built Dunrozel in Farnham Lane and developed land in the Hindhead area.

Not to be outdone, Lady Agatha, equally enchanted by the pines and heather, built herself a house called Rozeldene on the Headley Road, Hindhead, later to become the estate of the same name. Rozel was the name of the Russells' estate in pre-conquest Normandy.

Bertrand Russell was a frequent visitor to Dunrozel, where he would meet scientist John Tyndall and also the Pearsall Smith family from Philadelphia. Bertie, an agnostic, would eventually marry their younger daughter Alys, consenting to a Quaker marriage ceremony held at the Quaker Meeting Hall, Westminster. Neither Lady Russell, who disapproved of the marriage, nor any of his close relations attended, but the couple continued on to Holland for their honeymoon.

They moved into a workman's cottage built in the 16th century at Fernhurst and there Bertie wrote his first book *German Social Democracy*. Sadly the marriage failed despite numerous attempts to cure Alys' melancholy at a Brighton clinic.

It was here that Russell began his attack on the logical basis of mathematics, the first fruit of which was *The Principles of Mathematics*. Growing doubts over the underlying logic he used left him feeling dissatisfied, leading to publication of *Principia Mathematica*.

In order to concentrate on his writing he moved with Alys to Ivy Lodge at Tilford, but personal relations were at their lowest ebb, Bertie having no feelings whatsoever above duty to Alys.

He moved away from the area but did return to Abinger in Surrey much later to pursue his philosophical writings. Lady Ottoline featured in his romantic associations, but she also featured in the affairs of Roger Fry, Henry Lamb and Augustus John, also an acquaintance of Russell. When Bertie came on the scene these other love affairs were not over.

Later his unpopular Aunt Gertrude ran the Punch Bowl Inn at Hindhead. Bertie was married four times and eventually became the third Lord Russell.

DUNROZEL

GEORGE BERNARD SHAW
1856-1950

Shaw married Charlotte Payne-Townshend in 1898 and they rented Pitfold House between Shottermill and Hindhead. Shaw was not well, an infected bone in his foot making it necessary to use crutches until he was compelled to summon a London bone specialist. A small piece of bone was removed and after Charlotte took him off to the Isle of Wight, he returned to Pitfold a much healthier man.

Invigorated by the climate he completed *Caesar and Cleopatra* and began *Captain Brassbound's Conversion* here. He was revelling in the tranquility of the place and began cycling a great deal and he and Charlotte decided to move to a much larger house Blen Cathra in Hindhead, now St Edmund's School.

Shaw became involved in several local activities, the disarmament debate and natural history and he was, for a time, the music critic for the Farnham and Haslemere Herald, a local paper which is still going strong. The controversial Shaw gave a short talk to a local school and advised the children to disobey parents and grown ups where possible. The staff were distraught.

In 1899 the Shaws left Blen Cathra to tour Cornwall and then cruise the Mediterranean. By 1900 Shaw was spending occasional nights at the Beacon Hotel in Hindhead, taking a lease on Blackdown Cottage, which though more remote and secluded than previous properties, gave him the peace and stability to write *Three Plays for Puritans*. Before he had even seen it, Shaw had given the cottage a part in *Mrs Warren's Profession* as the setting for the first scene.

A library and refreshment house was a communal project supported by Shaw and his colleagues in Grayshott and Haslemere villages. Shaw also donated works by Tolstoy, Wordsworth and others and a street sign to this development was painted by the notable artist Walter Crane, of the Arts and Crafts Movement who was a friend of Shaw and a member of the Royal Institute of Watercolour Painters.

One of the finest residences in Hindhead, a luxury villa owned by the founder of Tarleton's underwear, was to feature in Shaw's 1909 play *Misalliance*. He could not have failed to notice that, 10 or 20 years earlier, the house would have been owned by a literary person, not a businessman.

BLEN CATHRA

EDMUND SPENSER
1552-1599

Gloriana was the title given to Queen Elizabeth 1 by poet Edmund Spenser whose attachment to the Queen and her court remained strong throughout his life. His great work *The Faerie Queene*, dedicated to the monarch, is the longest poem in the English language. Spenser received a Royal pension of £50 a year for his troubles, but had to wait many years before receiving the recognition he deserved. *The Faerie Queene*, intended as an historical allegory, celebrates the Elizabethan age but is full of veiled allusions to characters of the time.

Poets of his time were mostly aristocrats but Spenser's talent was such that, despite being Elizabethan middle class, he became a member of the literary group headed by patron Sir Philip Sidney and friends. Shakespeare apart, Edmund Spenser held the greatest reputation in literary circles of the age.

Spenser was just seven years old when Elizabeth 1 was crowned. He lived in Alton in a gable-fronted house in Amery Street near the market square, the house marked today by a small bronze plaque above the doorway. When he was 27 he published his *Shepherd's Calendar,* 12 poems dedicated to Sidney and a year later he was secretary to Lord Grey in Ireland, where he stayed for much of his life.

The 1590s was a very prolific time with the publication of a second set of three books of *The Faerie Queene* followed by *Amoretti* and *Epithalamion* and then *Prothalamion* and the *Fowre Hymnes,* all published by Ponsonby. It is thought Spenser returned to England in 1591 to oversee publication of *The Tears of the Muses,* residing for some of the time in Alton and writing *The Ruins of Time.*

English printers were kept very busy with the demand from Elizabethans and books at this time were often circulated in manuscript stage before the printing, which would often be done years later. There is no surviving manuscript of any part of *The Faerie Queene.*

The Stationers' Company, incorporated in 1557, dictated the terms of the printing and publishing trade. Books could be censored to prevent the publication of subversive material. Penalties were imposed to prevent books coming in from abroad and being printed in un-licensed premises. Licences were issued by six members of the Privy Council, usually the author supervising the printing, proof reading and corrections which were carried out in the printing works. The maximum number of copies allowed by the Stationers' Company was 1,250 and if a further edition was required and permission given the whole book had to be typeset again to spread the work among the printers.

AMERY STREET, ALTON

JONATHAN SWIFT
1667-1745

Jonathan Swift, a relative of Lady Dorothy Temple, arrived at Moor Park House, Farnham in 1691 as secretary and amanuensis to Sir William Temple, a notable statesman whose essay style was a prime influence on Swift. He was just 22 and was to stay, on and off, for 10 years. Paid an annual salary of £20 it is here that he wrote *A Tale of a Tub*, *A Discourse Concerning the Mechanical Operation of the Spirit* and *The Battle of Books*.

A widow, Mrs Bridget Johnson and her three children came to live in what is now known as Stella's Cottage, a charming house set back by the river near the entrance to the ruins of Waverley Abbey, a short walk from Moor Park House.

Swift became very attached to Hetty, one of Mrs Johnson's daughters and he undertook some of the child's education. 20 years later he would call her Stella and immortalise her in his writings.

It is easy to imagine the secretary/tutor and Stella, walking in the formal gardens of Moor Park House, she listening to Swift's philosophical outpourings. Swift was to leave Temple's employment on two occasions and when he returned to Moor Park House in 1696, he described Hetty, now 15, as 'having hair blacker than a raven, and every feature of her face perfection'.

When Sir William Temple died in 1699 he left his secretary £100 and the right to any profits made by the posthumous publication of Temple's books. Swift duly compiled his employer's papers and published them in two volumes.

Swift's cousin was rector of Puttenham Church at this time, so we can be sure that Jonathan was an occasional, if not a frequent visitor to the village.

Swift finally moved to Ireland and involved himself in a highly complex relationship with Stella and one Hester Vanhomrigh, but throughout these affairs he continued his creative writing. His attitude was not to marry until he was able to support a family, but at 49 he was still in debt. According to popular opinion, though there is no evidence, a few years after his appointment to the Deanery Swift and Stella were secretly married by St George Ashe, Bishop of Clogher in 1716.

Gulliver's Travels, his world-famous satire, was first published in October 1726 and has delighted readers ever since. Moor Park House is now a private residence and school with a section of the outbuildings devoted to the Constance Spry Flower School.

MOOR PARK HOUSE

ALFRED LORD TENNYSON
1809-1892

The Tennysons, Lord Alfred and his wife Emily, were encouraged to buy property in the area by Anne Gilchrist. They had taken a two year lease on Grayshott Farm while they searched, finally settling on a 36 acre site with a magnificent view on the eastern side of Blackdown, the land purchased for £1,400 from their new neighbour Lord Egmont.

Building began in 1868, the foundation stone laid on Shakespeare's birthday and Alfred and Emily moved in the following year. But with no road and no post, at times they found the isolation difficult. Egmont had refused their application for an access road and with unfinished stables even riding was impossible.

The study was decorated with marble figures of Roman emperors, and a wide corridor ran the whole length of the ground floor, in order that Alfred might take his daily walk even when the weather was unkind.

Some have seen the architect James Knowles' design for Aldworth as a version of his Grosvenor Hotel. The house would eventually serve the Poet Laureate well, providing the solitude essential for his work. Tennyson enjoyed walking his dogs around the Hindhead Punch Bowl, carrying a whistle to ward off any hikers who might stop his train of thought as the next poem took shape. He may have been concentrating hard, but because he was shortsighted he often surprised friends by not recognising them.

Tennyson died at Aldworth, a volume of Shakespeare open on his chest at the fifth act of *Cymbeline*. He had asked for it in response to a message from his sickly Emily at a time when he was supposed to be unable to see let alone read. The coffin was transported to Haslemere station by wagonette covered in flowers and thence to Westminster Abbey.

At one stage Tennyson had himself mesmerised but he had ability himself in this area and as a hypnotist managed to cure his wife's pain and sleeplessness for a few days. In 1882 he was concerned with the founding of the Society of Psychical Research. He also finally accepted an honour from the Queen and became Baron Tennyson of Aldworth and Freshwater.

Tennyson was a great admirer of Jane Austen, comparing her to Thackeray and Shakespeare. A sculpture of Tennyson by G F Watts from Compton in Surrey, stands on its plinth outside Lincoln Cathedral and at the Watts Gallery in Compton the plaster and maquette for this large work can be seen. There is also a water colour portrait of Tennyson by Helen Allingham, member of the Royal Watercolour Society, who lived at Witley and is famous for her rural landscapes and cottages of this area.

A fine bronze of Lord Tennyson now sits gazing over the view towards Sussex and the coast much loved by the author. This was installed by the present owner who has restored the property to its former glory. Unfortunately it cannot be seen from the road.

ALDWORTH

IZAAK WALTON
1593-1683

Izaak Walton was steward of Farnham Castle and author of *The Compleat Angler* or *The Contemplative Man's Recreation: being a discourse of fish and fishing*, a book which has stayed in print ever since it first appeared in 1653, to be largely rewritten for the second edition two years later.

Born in Stafford, he was apprenticed to a draper and was a staunch loyalist during the Civil War. He lost his house near St Paul's in the Great Fire of London. More than just a writer of pastoral themes, Walton is one of the fathers of literary biography, writing portraits of the likes of John Donne, George Herbert and Richard Hooker.

Whenever he crossed the River Wey by the footbridge he noted that the river had some of the finest fish in the area. Author Charles Kingsley had noticed too and often came to Farnham for the excellent fishing, staying with his friend John Mainwaring Payne.

The Compleat Angler combines practical information on angling with folklore, quotations, pastoral interludes of songs and ballads, and glimpses of an idyllic rural life of well-kept inns and tuneful milkmaids.

Until 1927 the Castle was the residence of the Bishops of Winchester who were very wealthy and often entertained kings and their extensive retinues. King John stayed 18 times at the Castle, so one can assume the hunting was good in the area. Henry I, Henry III, Edward I, Edward II, Richard III, Henry VII and Henry VIII all took advantage of the resident Bishop's hospitality. This created plenty of work for the town with accompanying displays of pageantry.

The constant streams of visitors caused each successive Bishop to extend the building, and in the 15th century Bishop Waynflete added the large tower with its distinctive diaper brick pattern.

During the Civil War the Castle was held by Royalists but on behalf of the Parliamentarians Colonel Sir William Waller stormed the Castle and during this period the town of Farnham became a centre for the garrison.

The original Castle Keep is now administered by English National Heritage and open from April to September and the view of the ancient town of Farnham is well worth the climb. The main part of the building is now a Centre for International Briefing and from time to time concerts are held in the Castle.

By the time *The Life of Richard Hooker* was published in 1670, Walton was living in the Close at Winchester as Bishop Morley's steward. But he had not forgotten his time at Farnham. At the age of 90, he was to write his last piece of prose - his will. Witnessed and sealed with the bloodstone seal given him by John Donne, it is a document which bears witness to what every reader except Byron agreed upon, his kindness.

'...and I give my dafter Doctor Halls Works which be now at Farnham.......to my son Izaak I give all my books (not yet given) at Farnham Castell and a deske of prints and pikters; also a cabinet nere my beds head, in which are som littell things that he will valew, tho of noe great worth.'

FARNHAM CASTLE

H G WELLS
1866-1946

As a child Herbert George Wells was an avid reader at the local literary institute and library. He was apprenticed to a firm of drapers in Windsor, then acted as a pupil teacher at a school in Somerset. In 1884 he was awarded a scholarship to the Imperial College of Science, South Kensington and studied among other subjects, biology with Professor Thomas Huxley (Aldous Huxley's grandfather). In 1890 he took a BSc degree with first class honours in zoology at London University.

He began to write essays and reviews for periodicals, and then wrote *The Time Machine* and *The Wonderful Visit*, two books which established his reputation as an imaginative writer. In 1895 he married Catherine Robbins, a former student, his first marriage being previously dissolved.

In the following years he produced *The War of the Worlds, The Invisible Man* and a whole series of brilliant scientific romances, which firmly established his worldwide reputation as an author. Throughout, his concern was with the development of materials. If the human race did not control their production, then it would perish, he maintained.

After a short time living in Woking with his new wife in 1895, Wells spent most of his life at Sandgate near Folkestone but in 1911 he occupied Cochet Farm, west of Blackdown, near Haslemere in order to continue his writing in peace and quiet. The novel on which he was then working was probably *Marriage*, the successor to *The New Machiavelli*.

But work alone was not it seems the only motive for going to Cochet. He had already met a widow Elizabeth von Arnim in London whose sister lived on the eastern outskirts of Fernhurst. The pair soon came to 'an easy understanding', walking frequently in the Devil's Punch Bowl.

Some at least of *The Marriage* was written during his sojourn at Cochet, a story with impeccable morals. Although it can be assumed that Elizabeth found Wells entertaining company after her rather boring late husband, Wells would never allow associations of this sort to interfere with his work. Elizabeth was soon to be replaced when the young Rebecca West wrote a destructive review of the novel and acquired instant appeal in Wells' eyes.

Cochet Farm is in a delightful, secluded valley of wild life and flowers. The inglenook fireplace is an important feature and the wealth of oak beams in the house gives a timeless atmosphere to the building. Some restoration of the stone mullion windows has been carried out in a sensitive manner.

COCHET FARM

GILBERT WHITE
1720-1793

The village of Selborne is much as it was in Gilbert White's days. In the main street is a rich variety of country architecture, thatched, timber and brick, all charmingly surrounded by small hills called 'hangers'. Understandably the village has become something of a mecca for those interested in natural history, with many delightful walks including the zig-zag walk, created by Gilbert White and his brother.

Gilbert White was born in the vicarage at Selborne and studied at Oxford gaining a B.A. at Oriel College. The success of his book *The Natural History of Selborne* is largely due to his skilled and direct observation of animal behaviour and the growth of plants from one season to another.

Turning his back on Oxford when they rejected his application for Provost of Oriel College, Gilbert turned his attentions to his home and parish, and in particular to the magnificent garden of his house, previously called The Wakes. He grew some 50 different vegetable varieties including the newly introduced maize, wild rice and potatoes.

White pioneered the observation of natural history, able to recognise the difference in birds with similar plumage simply by the variations of their birdsong. He also discovered the harvest mouse as a separate species, the research involving pickling them in brandy for further investigation.

It is the simplicity of Gilbert White's diaries and records that create immediate appeal. Reading the Gilbert White *Garden Kalendar,* his first formal journal, is to compare the differences in wild life habits across two and a half centuries. In November 1758 he looked out over the meadow behind the house and was astonished to see a late flock of house-martins, a bird that does not just share human homes, but behaves like 'a careful workman'.

First curate at Farringdon and then curate-in-charge at Selborne, Gilbert built extensions at his Selbourne house and enlisted the help of many local people in compiling *The Natural History*. His house is open to the public during summer months and includes an extensive bookshop specialising in works of natural history. Extensive work in the garden has involved research and re-planting with flowers and vegetables that grew in Gilbert White's times.

His diaries are full of little observations. On October 25 1783 he states 'on the King's accession the guns fired at Portsmouth and shook the windows of the house at Selborne'.

In the grounds of the ancient church nearby are the remains of the famous Yew tree, damaged in the great storm of 1987. Apart from the delightful church architecture the altarpiece is exceptional, painted by Jan Mostaert (1475-1555), the Netherlandish artist.

GILBERT WHITE'S HOUSE

INDEX

Abinger 30
Agatha, Lady 30
Aldworth 30, 38
Allah-Akbarries 10
Allen, Grant 20
Allingham, Helen 38
Alton 8, 26
Amery Street, Alton 34
Ashe, St George 36
Aunt Gertrude 30
Austen, Cassandra 8
Austen, Edward 8
Austen, Jane 8, 38
Austen, Sir Frances 8

Ball, Henry 20
Barrie, James 10, 20
Beacon Hotel 32
Bell, Clive 28
Belper 22
Bennett, Arnold 12
Bermondsey 18
Bettesworth, Fred 12
Bishop Morley 40
Bishop Waynflete 40
Black Lake Cottage 10
Blackdown 24, 38, 42
Blackdown Cottage 32
Blen Cathra 32
Bloemfontein 20
Bloomsbury Group 28
Bourne, George 12
Brighton clinic 30
Bronte, Charlotte 26
Browning 24
Burne Jones 24
Byron, Lord 40

Captain W E Johns 22
Carlyle, Sir Thomas 26
Carroll, Lewis 14
Charterhouse 28
Cheshire 26
Chestnuts 14
Chopin 24
Civil War 40
Cobbett, William 16
Cochet Farm 42
Compton 28, 38
Conan Doyle, Jean 20
Conan Doyle, Louise 20
Conan Doyle, Sir Arthur 10
Cornwall 32
Crane, Walter 32
Cross, John 24
Crown Inn 18
Curtis Museum 18
Curtis, Samuel 18
Curtis, Thomas 18
Curtis, William 18

Darnell, Dorothy 8
Derbyshire 22
Devil's Punch Bowl 42
Dickens, Charles 26
Dodgson, Reverend Charles
  Lutwidge 14
Donne, John 40
Doyle, Sir Arthur Conan 20
Dunrozel 30

Edinburgh 20
Edward l 40
Edward ll 40
Edwards, Monica 22
Edwards, Sydenham 18

Egmont, Lord 38
Eliot, George 24
English National Heritage 40
Eton 28
Evans, Mary Ann 24

Farnham 16, 40
Farnham Castle 40
Farnham Lane 30
Farnham Museum 16
Farringdon 44
Fernhurst 30, 42
Folkestone 42
Fry, Roger 30
Fuller, Audrey 14

Gaskell, Elizabeth 26
Gaskell, William 26
Gervas 28
Gielgud, Lewis 28
Gielgud, Sir John 28
Gilchrist, Anne 38
Girtler, Mark 28
Gloriana 34
Godalming 28
Goldmersham Park 8
Grace, WG 20
Grant, Duncan 28
Graves, Robert 28
Graves, William 18
Grayshott 32
Grayshott Farm 38
Great Fire of London 40
Great Ormond Street Hospital 14
Grey, Lord 34
Grosvenor Hotel 38
Grover, Freddie 12
Guildford 14

Guildford Museum 14

Hansard 16
Haslemere 30, 32, 38, 42
Hazlitt, William 16
Headley Road 30
Henry l 40
Henry lll 40
Henry Vll 40
Henry Vlll 40
Herbert, George 40
Highgate Cemetery 24
Hillside School 28
Hindhead 20, 30, 32
Hog's Back 16
Holland 30
Holland, Sir Henry 24
Holman Hunt 14
Holmes, Sherlock 20
Holybourne 26
Hooker, Richard 40
HRH The Prince of Wales 28
Hughes, Arthur 14
Huntington Library 14
Huxley, Aldous 28
Huxley, Julia 28
Huxley, Leonard, 28
Huxley, Professor Thomas 42

Imperial College of Science,
  South Kensington 42
Ireland 34, 36
Ivy Lodge, Tilford 30

Jane Austen Society 8
John, Augustus 30
Johnson, Hetty 36
Johnson, Mrs Bridget 36

Jolly Farmer Inn 16

King John 40
Kingsley, Charles 40
Knowles, James 38
Knutsford 26

Lamb, Henry 30
Lambeth Marsh 18
Lawrence, D H 28
Legg, John 18
Lenten Street, Alton 18
Lewes, George Henry 24
Lincoln Cathedral 38
Llewellyn Davies 10
Lobswood Club 10
Locker, Eleanor 24
London 20
London University 42

Macmillan 14
Mainwaring Payne, John 40
Manchester 26
MCC 20
Mediterranean 32
MGM 28
Millais 14
Moor Park House 36
Morris, William 12
Mostaert, Jan 44

National Rifle Association 20
Natural History Museum 28
Newdigate Prison 16
Normandy 16
Normandy, France 30

Oriel College, Oxford 44

Ottoline, Lady 28, 30
Oxford 28

Paris 26
Payne-Townshend, Charlotte 32
Pearsall Smith, Alys 30
Pearsall Smiths 30
Philadelphia 30
Pitfold House 32
Plague 18
Poet's Corner 24
Ponsonby 34
Porcupine, Peter 16
Portsmouth 20, 44
Princess Beatrice 14
Princess Louise, Marchioness of
    Lorne 24
Prior's Field 28
Prior's Field School 28
Punch Bowl 28, 38
Punch Bowl Farm 22
Punch Bowl Inn 30
Puttenham Church 36

Quaker Meeting Hall 30
Queen Elizabeth l 34
Queen Victoria 14

Rich, Robert 16
Richard lll 40
River Wey 14, 40
Robbins, Catherine 42
Romney Marsh 22
Rossetti 14
Royal Gardens, Kew 16
Royal Watercolour Society 38
Rozel 30
Rozeldene 30

Russell, Bertrand 28, 30
Rye Harbour 22

Sandgate 42
Sands, George 24
Sanson, Francis 18
Schumann, Clara 24
Scott, Sir Giles Gilbert 28
Selborne 18, 44
Sele Common 16
Shakespeare, William 34, 38
Shaw, George Bernard 32
Shottermill 32
Sidney, Sir Philip 34
Society of Psychical Research 38
Somerset 42
Southsea 20
Sowerby, James 18
Spenser, Edmund 34
Spry, Constance 36
St. Paul's, London 40
St. Edmund's School 32
St. George's Church, Hanover
    Square 24
St. James Gazette 14
Stafford 40
Stationers' Company 34
Stella's Cottage 36
Sturt, George 12
Swift, Jonathan 36

Temple, Lady Dorothy 36
Temple, Sir William 36
Tenniel 14
Tennyson, Emily 38
Tennyson, Lionel 24
Tennyson, Lord Alfred 24, 38
Terry, Ellen 14

Thackeray, William 38
The Heights 24
The Lawn 26
The Wakes 44
Thursley 22
Tolstoy 32
Tyndall, John 30

Uncle Rollo 30
Undershaw 20
Undershaw Hotel and
    Restaurant 20
Undershaw Rifle Club 20

Vanhomrigh, Hester 36
Vine Cottage 12
Von Armin, Elizabeth 42
Voysey, Charles 28

Waller, Sir William 40
Walton, Izaak 40
Watson, Doctor 20
Watts Gallery 38
Watts GF 38
Watts Memorial Chapel 28
Waverley 16
Waverley Abbey 36
Waverley Abbey House 16
Wells, HG 28, 42
West, Rebecca 42
Westminster Abbey 24, 38
White, Gilbert 18, 44
Williamson, Henry 12
Windsor 42
Witley 24, 38
Woking 42
Woolf, Virginia 28
Wordsworth, William 32